We Like Bugs!

by Frankie Hartley • illustrated by Jan Bryan Hunt

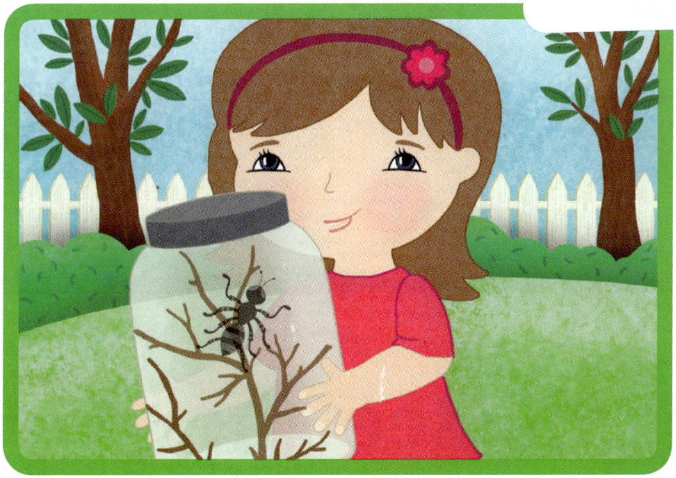

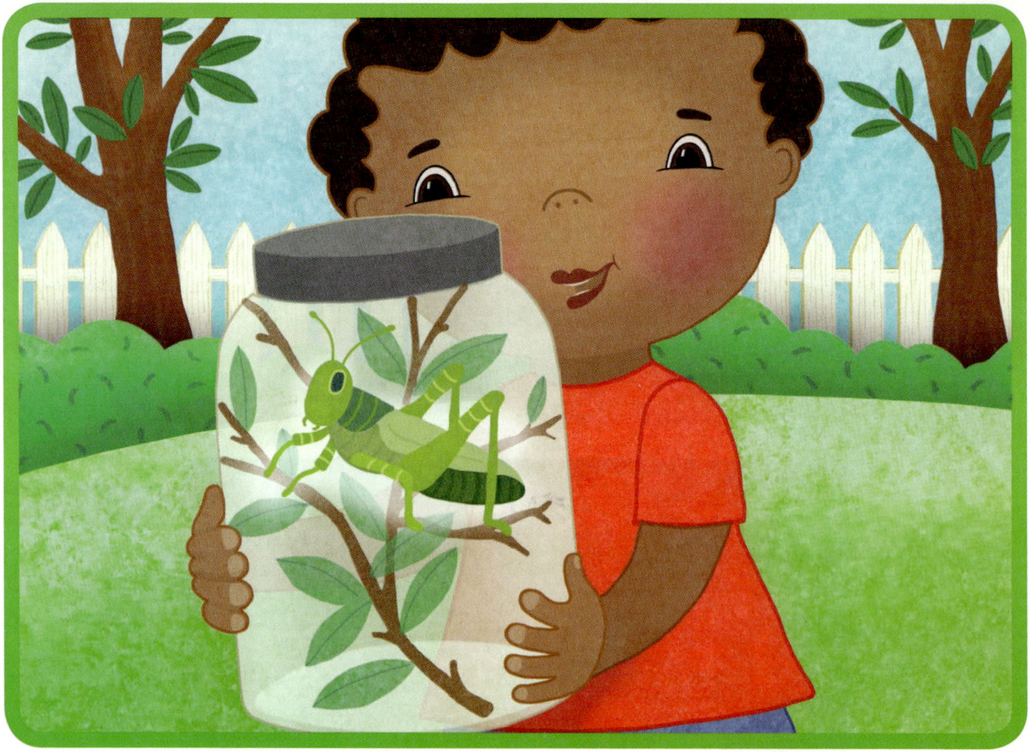

Can you see the 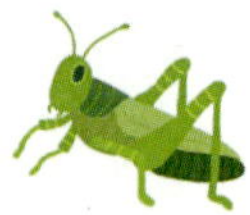 grasshopper ?

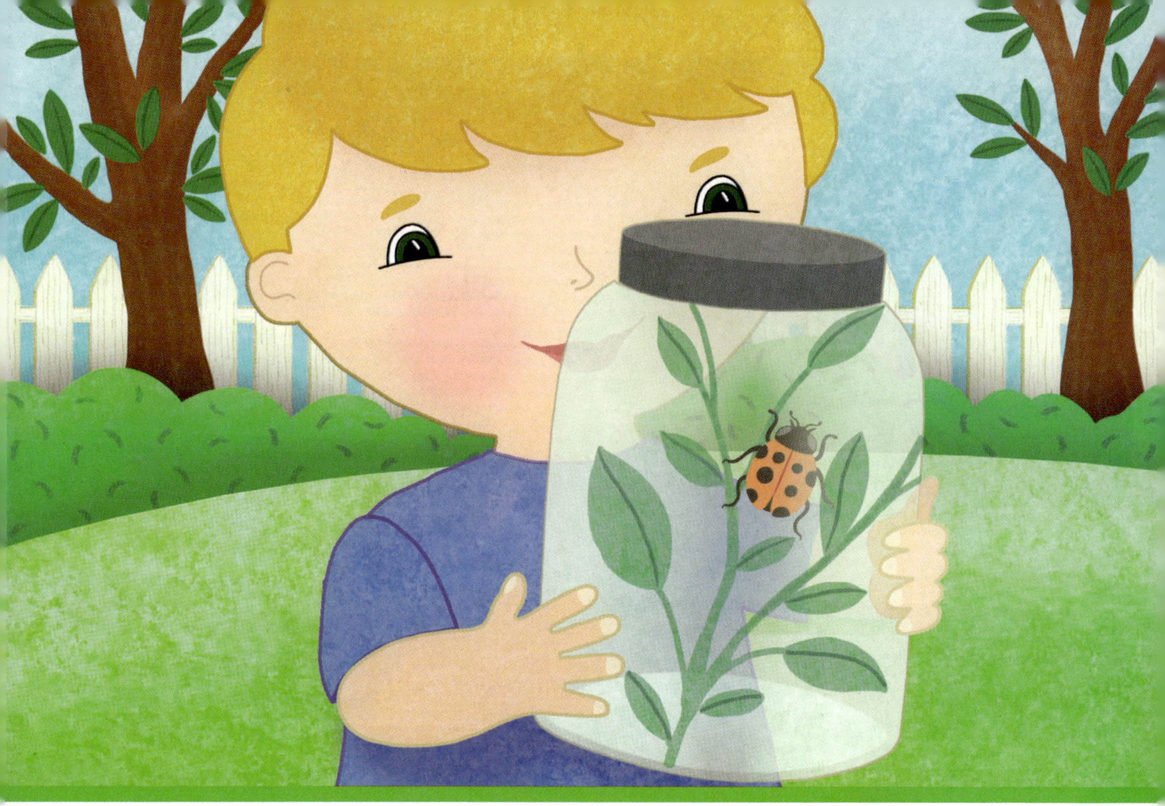

Can you see the 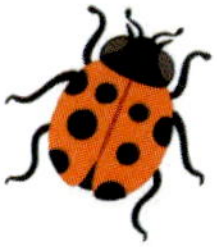 ladybug?

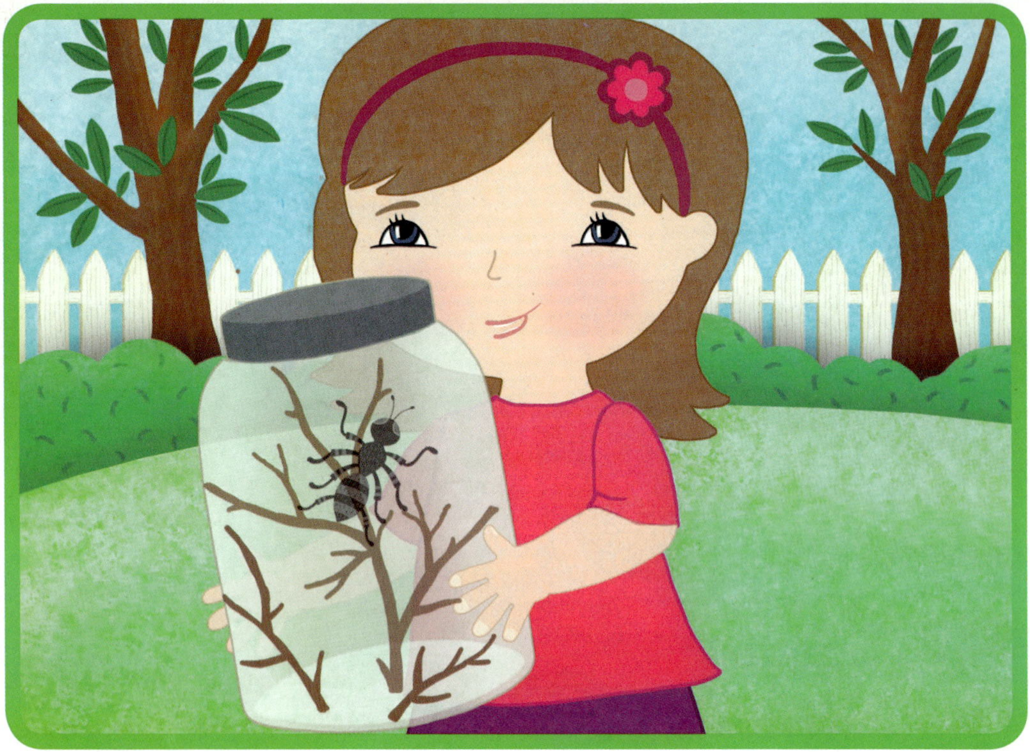

Can you see the 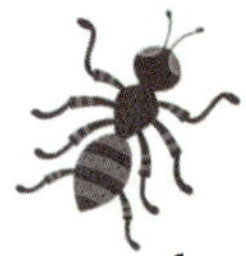 ant ?

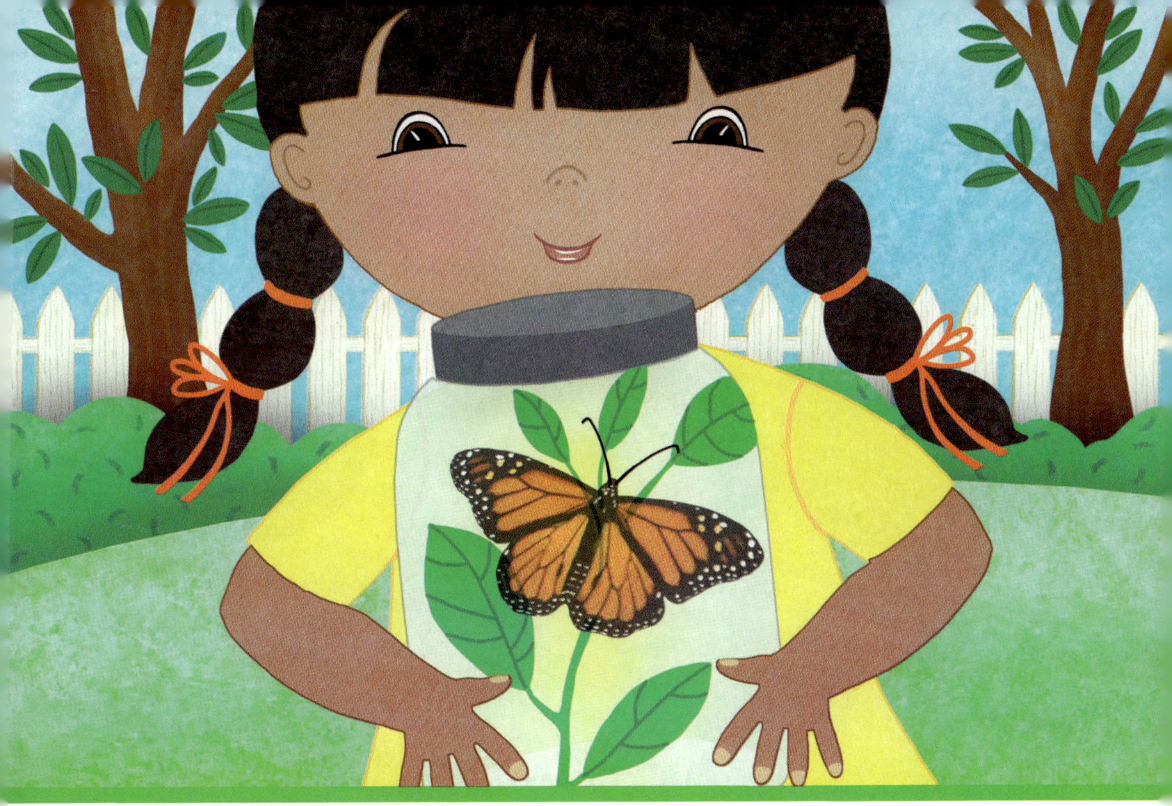

Can you see the 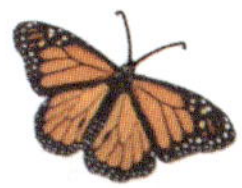 butterfly?

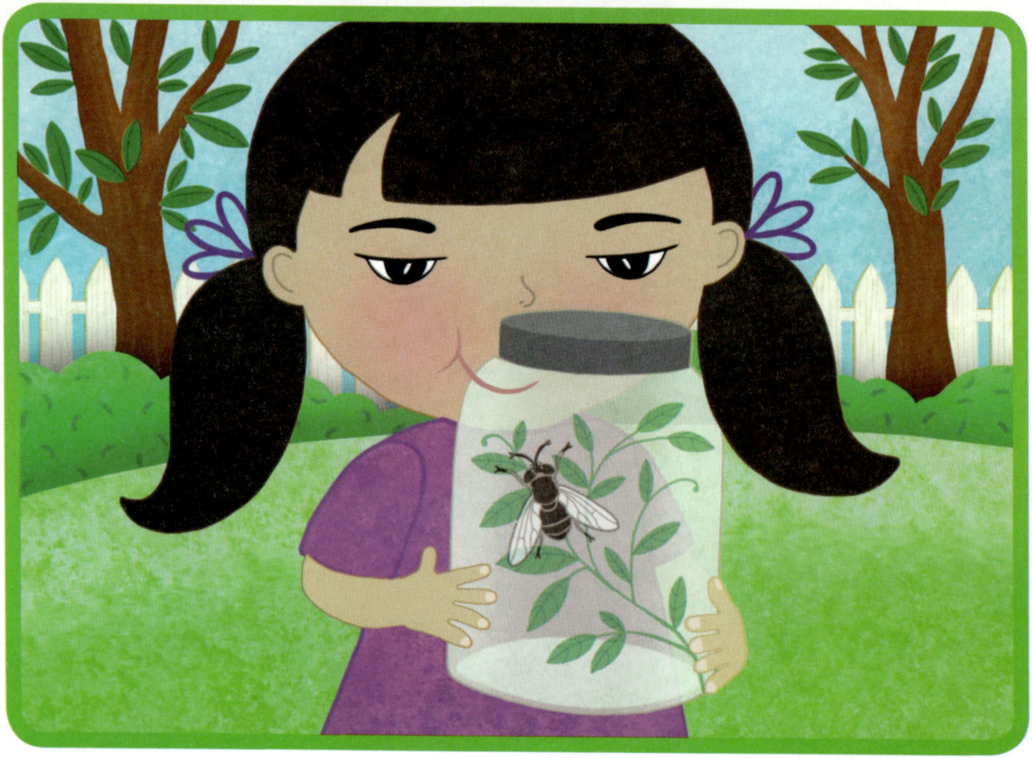

Can you see the 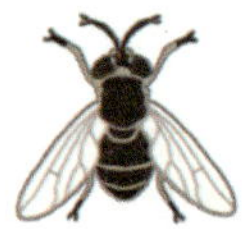 fly ?

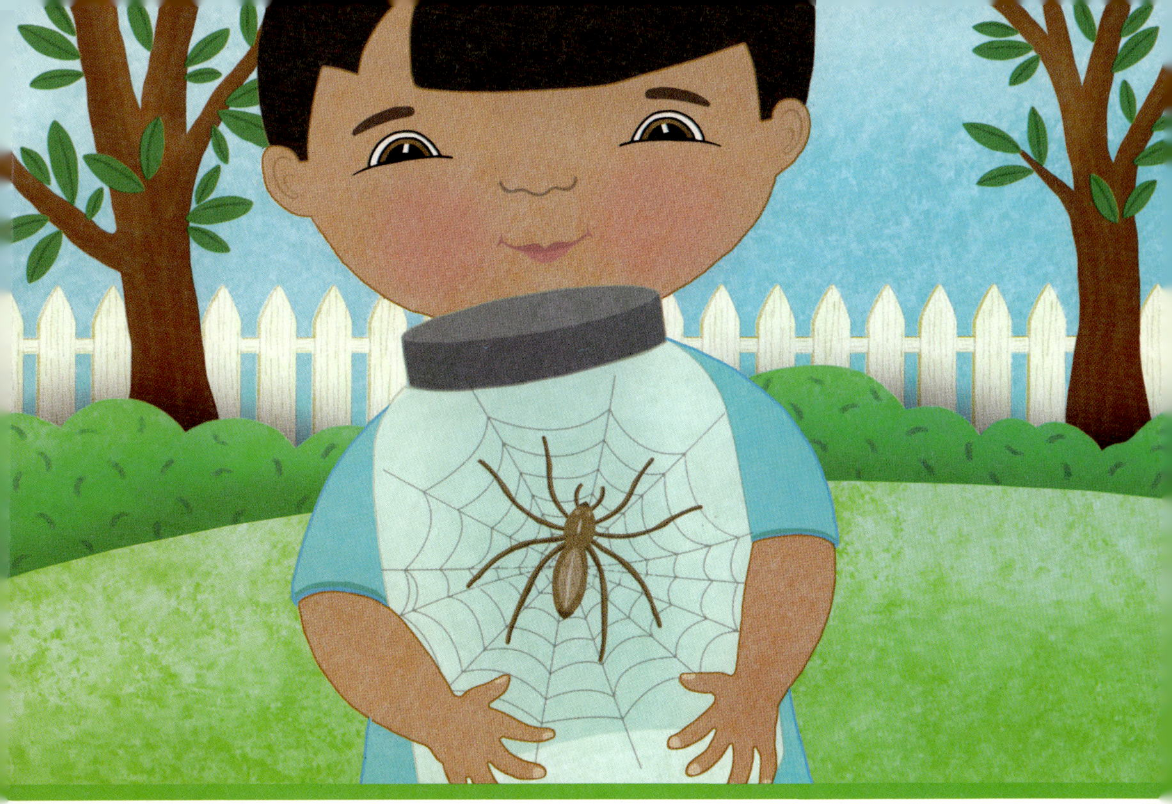

Can you see the 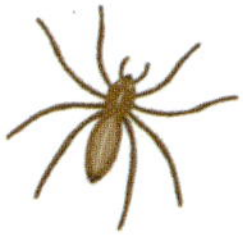 spider ?

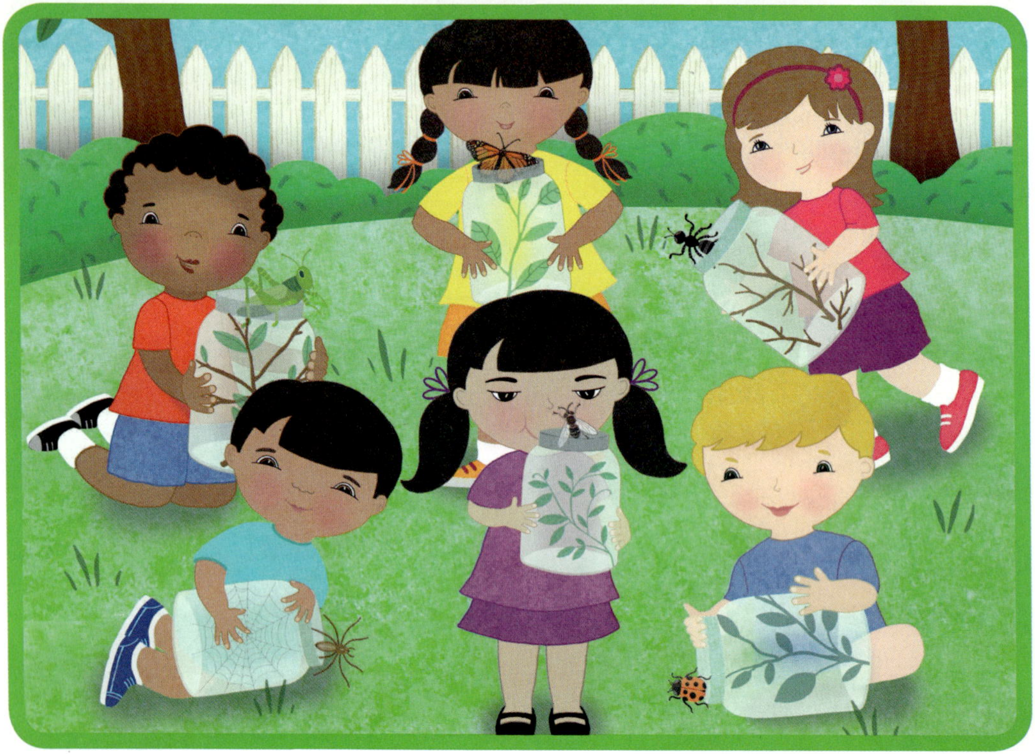

We can see the 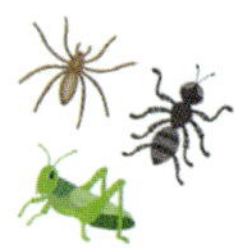 bugs !